SWALLOWTAIL BUTTERFLIES

SWALLOWTAIL BUTTERFLIES

by Jane Dallinger and Cynthia Overbeck

Photographs by Yuko Sato

A Lerner Natural Science Book

Lerner Publications Company ▪ Minneapolis

Sylvia A. Johnson, Series Editor

Translation of original text by Kay Kushino

The publisher wishes to thank Ronald L. Huber, Entomologist,
The Science Museum of Minnesota, and Jerry W. Heaps,
Department of Entomology, The University of Minnesota,
for their assistance in the preparation of this book.

The glossary on page 46 gives definitions and pronunciations
of words shown in **bold type** in the text.

LIBRARY OF CONGRESS CATALOGING IN PUBLICATION DATA

Dallinger, Jane.
  Swallowtail butterflies.

    (A Lerner natural science book)
    Adaptation of: Agehachō/by Noboru Motofuji.
    Includes index.
    Summary: Introduces the various butterflies found
  in all parts of the world that have in common a slender
  pointed tip, or tail, on each hindwing.
    1. Papilionidae—Juvenile literature. [1. Swallowtail
  butterflies. 2. Butterflies] I. Overbeck, Cynthia. II. Satō,
  Yūkō, 1928-   ., ill. III. Motofuji, Noboru. Agehachō.
  IV. Title. V. Series.

  QL561.P2D34   595.78′9   82-15294
  ISBN 0-8225-1465-6 (lib. bdg.)   AACR2

International Standard Book Number: 0-8225-1465-6
Library of Congress Catalog Card Number: 82-15294

1 2 3 4 5 6 7 8 9 10 91 90 89 88 87 86 85 84 83 82

Two different kinds of swallowtail butterflies. The picture on the right shows the long tails on the wings that give these butterflies their common name.

Butterflies, along with their close relatives moths, are insects that make up the scientific order Lepidoptera (lehp-ih-DOP-tih-ra). This Latin word means "scale-wing," and it describes a butterfly's most noticeable feature—its beautiful, delicate wings. There are about 24,000 different species, or kinds, of butterflies, and each has its own unique wing color and pattern.

Swallowtail butterflies have a special wing feature that no other butterflies have. On each hindwing is a slender, pointed tip or tail. Swallowtails were given their common name because these "tails" reminded people of the long, pointed wings of the birds called swallows.

Here are just a few of the different kinds of swallowtail butterflies that live in many parts of the world. Their common English names are given along with their species names. These Latin names are recognized by scientists everywhere, no matter what language they speak. *Top left:* Black swallowtail *(Papilio demetrius). Top right:* Oasis swallowtail *(Graphium sarpedon). Bottom left:* Monkey swallowtail *(Papilio helenus). Bottom right:* Black crow swallowtail *(Atrophaneura alcinous).*

An Old World swallowtail (*Papilio machaon*)

Although swallowtails have wings with a special shape, their basic body structure is the same as that of other butterflies. Like all insects, a butterfly's body is made up of three parts: the head, the **thorax**, and the **abdomen.**

On a butterfly's head are two large eyes and two long, thin sense organs called **antennae.** Each antenna is tipped with a tiny knob. Butterflies use their antennae to detect the odors of flowers, which contain their main food, a sweet liquid called **nectar.**

To get nectar from its storage place within a flower, a butterfly uses its **proboscis.** This is a long tube that extends from the butterfly's mouth. When it is not being used, the proboscis rests in a rolled-up position under the insect's head. A butterfly can extend its proboscis deep into a flower in order to suck out the nectar. Butterflies also drink water through this tube. But a butterfly does not use its proboscis to taste its food. Its taste organs are located on the bottoms of its feet.

The thorax is the middle part of a butterfly's body, and connected to it are three pairs of legs and two pairs of wings. Located on the back section, or abdomen, are eight pairs of breathing holes, or **spiracles.**

A butterfly's two pairs of wings are made of a thin skin that is supported by a framework of veins. The skin itself is transparent and has no color. The color comes from thousands of **scales** that cover the wings' surfaces. These tiny particles are arranged in an overlapping fashion, much like

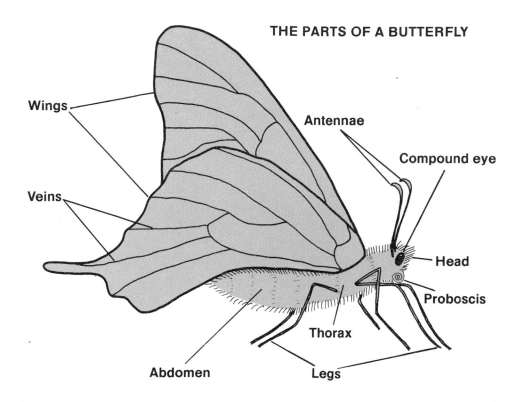

THE PARTS OF A BUTTERFLY

Wings

Veins

Antennae

Compound eye

Head

Proboscis

Thorax

Abdomen

Legs

shingles on a house. They are so small and delicate that they will brush right off the wings like colored dust. Yet they create brilliant colors and designs.

Butterfly scales produce color in two different ways. Some scales contain chemicals called **pigments** that produce the colors red, orange, yellow, or brown. Other scales have surfaces that act like a prism to bend and scatter light rays. As light hits these scales, it is bent and reflected off in many directions. When rays of light are bent in certain ways, the colors of blue, violet, or green appear. Both kinds of scales may be mixed together on one wing.

This magnified picture shows how water forms beads on the surface of a butterfly's wing.

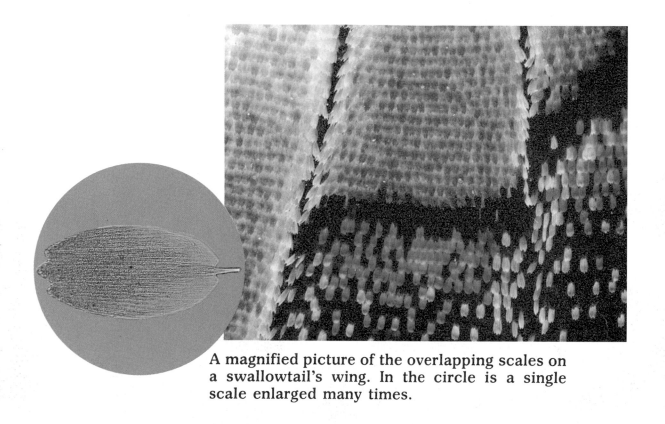

A magnified picture of the overlapping scales on a swallowtail's wing. In the circle is a single scale enlarged many times.

The scales on butterfly wings serve several very useful purposes. First, the colors and patterns they make help butterflies of the same species to identify one another. The covering of scales also protects a butterfly's wings by repelling water. As the picture on the opposite page shows, a drop of water beads up on the surface of the wing instead of soaking in. If water soaked into the wings, the butterfly would become too heavy to fly. Then it would not be able to find food or a mate. It would also be unable to fly away from **predators**—animals that would try to attack and eat it.

The patterns on this swallowtail's wings blend with the sunlight and shadow of the forest.

Butterflies have no weapons such as stingers or claws to defend themselves against predators. They usually depend on swift flight to escape their enemies. They also depend on **protective coloring.** This means that the colors and patterns of the butterfly's wings often blend in with the surroundings in such a way that the insect cannot easily be seen by birds and other predators.

The blue-green wings of the swallowtails in the picture on the opposite page blend in with leaves on the forest floor. Other swallowtails, like the one in the picture above, look conspicuous at first with their bright, patterned wings. But when they flutter through the sunlight and shadow of the forest, the light and dark patterns blend so well with the surroundings that the butterflies seem to disappear.

12

Predators might find it difficult to see these blue-green crow swallowtails against the background of the forest floor.

Protective coloring does not always keep butterflies out of danger. The giant swallowtail in this picture has just been captured by a praying mantis.

Despite their protective coloring and swift flight, many butterflies are attacked and eaten by predators. Even if they avoid such attacks, most butterflies live for only a few days or weeks. During this brief time, they feed only on flower nectar. Some have such short lives that they eat nothing at all in their adult stage. Monarch butterflies and a few other species need extra food because they have longer lives than most of their relatives. These butterflies live for several months and feed on the juice of rotten fruit as well as flower nectar.

A swallowtail butterfly usually lives for several weeks. During this time, the insect has only two important things to do: find food and find a mate.

Finding a mate is a very important part of the life cycle of a butterfly. Male and female butterflies must find partners of the opposite sex in order to reproduce. Like most insects, butterflies reproduce sexually. In the process of sexual reproduction, special sex cells from a male and a female butterfly unite to create new life.

Most butterflies go through the same basic activities in finding a mate. The males begin by searching for females of their species. Some male butterflies will fly over a large area, looking for a female. Others perch in a sunny spot on a tree, a bush, or in the grass and wait for a female to come near. Male swallowtails often choose a tree or rock on a hilltop.

A male butterfly will mate only with a female of his own species. He recognizes her by her distinctive wing colors and markings. If a butterfly of another species comes near, he chases it away. When a suitable female finally approaches, the male flies out to meet her. Sometimes several males approach one female. They all fly around her, trying to get her attention.

Left: A male and female swallowtail fly together, searching for a place to mate. *Opposite:* The butterflies mate on a twig.

Eventually the male and female butterflies form pairs. A pair may fly around for a while searching for a place to mate. Finally the two butterflies settle on a tree or bush. They mate by putting the tips of their abdomens together. The partners usually stay in this position for an hour or more. During this time, male sex cells, or sperm, pass from the male's body to the female's body. The sperm are enclosed in a kind of packet called a **spermatophore,** which is stored in the female's abdomen. Later the male butterfly's sperm will unite with, or fertilize, the egg cells produced in the female's body.

Opposite: A female swallowtail lays her eggs on a tree. In the circle is a single egg magnified many times.

When mating is over, the two butterflies separate. The male often flies away to search for another partner. The female usually will not mate a second time. Instead, she flies about for a day or two until she is ready to lay her eggs.

Many species of butterflies lay their eggs only on specific kinds of plants. These plants are the ones that the offspring will use for food when they hatch. The female swallowtail in the picture on the opposite page has chosen a Japanese shanso tree as the place to lay her eggs. Other swallowtails use willow, aspen, and laurel trees, as well as sagebrush or even carrot and celery plants. The sense organs on their feet help them to recognize the right plants.

When a female butterfly has found the plant she is seeking, she begins to lay her eggs. As each egg passes out of her body, it is fertilized by the sperm stored in her abdomen. Like many butterflies, a female swallowtail deposits her sticky eggs on the undersides of leaves or twigs. There they will be hidden from birds and insects. The eggs are not all laid in one place but are scattered around on different parts of the plant. That way, even if some are discovered, all will not be destroyed.

A female swallowtail usually lays about 100 eggs. Other kinds of butterflies lay anywhere from a few dozen eggs to as many as 1,500.

When a female butterfly lays her eggs, she starts the process of development that will eventually produce new adult butterflies. This remarkable process is called **metamorphosis,** a combination of Greek words meaning "transformation." A butterfly's metamorphosis is made up of four separate stages: egg, larva, pupa, and adult. Each stage is very different from all the others.

The egg stage of a swallowtail's metamorphosis lasts about a week. At the end of that time, the egg hatches. The bristly, worm-like creature that emerges is a **larva** or **caterpillar,** the second stage in the butterfly's development.

A swallowtail caterpillar hatches by chewing a hole in the soft covering of its egg (picture 1 on the opposite page). Once it has made a big enough hole, it slowly crawls out onto the leaf's underside (2). Immediately it begins to spin threads of silk (3). Silk is a substance produced by glands inside the larva's body. It comes out as a fine thread through tiny tubes called **spinnerets,** located near the larva's mouth.

The caterpillar attaches its silk thread to the underside of the leaf. The thread acts as a safety line to prevent the larva from falling off the slippery surface. After the caterpillar is completely free of its shell, it finishes spinning its silk. The silk now forms a tiny platform to which the caterpillar clings (4).

Soon after hatching, the caterpillar begins to eat its egg shell (5 and 6). The shell contains nutritious food that the larva needs to continue its development.

22

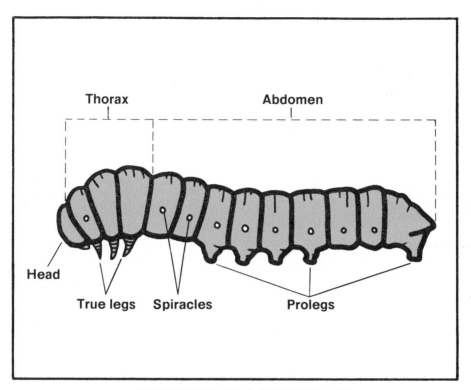

THE PARTS OF A CATERPILLAR

Like most butterfly larvae, the newly hatched swallowtail caterpillar is very small. It is so tiny that it can be seen clearly only with a magnifying glass. Its body consists of a head and 12 rounded sections, or segments. On the larva's head are six simple eyes capable only of telling the difference between light and dark. A larva also has a pair of small antennae and strong jaws designed for chewing. It breathes through tiny spiracles on the sides of its body.

Like all caterpillars, the swallowtail caterpillar has several different kinds of legs. The three pairs on the first three segments of its body are called **true legs**. They are jointed, with sharp claws at the tips. These legs will eventually become the six legs of the adult butterfly. Most caterpillars also have five pairs of false legs, or **prolegs.** These are stumpy, unjointed structures with groups of tiny hooks called **crochets** at the tips. This combination of legs enables the caterpillar to climb and crawl about on the leaves that supply its food.

This odd little creature has one purpose in life, and that is to eat. The larva must eat and grow in order to get ready for the next stage in its development. During the larval stage, the caterpillar will eat so much that it will grow to be seven or eight times as large as it was when it first hatched.

After eating its egg shell, the caterpillar begins feeding on the plant leaves around it. At first it can chew only tiny pinholes in the softest parts of the leaves. But soon it chews up whole leaves with ease.

If it is not attacked by predators, the caterpillar grows quickly on its leafy diet. Scientists divide its growth into five different stages, called **instars.** During each instar, the caterpillar becomes larger.

This caterpillar is in its second instar.

The first instar begins as soon as the caterpillar hatches from its egg. As the young caterpillar gobbles up leaves, its body grows rapidly. Unlike human skin, a larva's skin doesn't grow along with its body: it stays the same size. When the caterpillar becomes too large for its skin, it is time for a change.

The caterpillar stops eating temporarily. It begins to twist and squirm until its skin splits at the back. Then the caterpillar works its way out through the opening. Underneath, a new, larger layer of skin has been growing. The new skin soon hardens to protect the larva's soft body. This process of shedding old skin is called **molting**. After a caterpillar molts for the first time, it is about twice as big as its original size. Now it is called a second-instar larva.

After a few more days of eating, the caterpillar again grows too large for its skin. It molts and becomes a third-instar larva like the one shown on the opposite page.

26

The third instar is about three times as big as the first instar. Its appearance has also changed. The caterpillar's spines are now smaller, and its brownish-black skin is marked with white splotches. These white marks act as protective coloring. From a distance, they look something like bird droppings. Predators usually keep away from caterpillars with such unattractive markings.

Like most caterpillars, swallowtails molt four different times. The caterpillar shown in the picture on the left is going through its fourth molt. In the picture above, you can see the same caterpillar a few minutes after molting. It has turned around on the branch and is eating its old skin, which contains nutrients its body uses.

The caterpillar is now in its fifth and final instar, and its appearance is quite different from that of all the earlier instars.

A fifth-instar caterpillar

The final instar of the swallowtail caterpillar, shown on the opposite page, is a very exotic-looking creature. It has bright green skin with distinctive black, white, and yellow markings. Rising from behind its head is a strange kind of orange horn. All of these features play a role in defending the caterpillar from its many enemies.

The swallowtail's orange "horn" is its most unusual protective device. This structure is actually an organ known as an **osmeterium**. Normally the osmeterium is pulled back inside the caterpillar's body. But when a predator threatens to attack, the larva extends the forked organ, which is covered with a bad-smelling chemical. The smell released into the air is so unpleasant that it often drives the attacker away. Swallowtails are the only butterfly caterpillars to use this special method of self-defense.

Swallowtails have some defensive features that are shared by other kinds of caterpillars. Many caterpillars have bright green skins that blend in with the green leaves around them. Some caterpillars, including several species of swallowtails, also have markings on their bodies that actually frighten predators away. These markings are known as eyespots and usually appear behind the caterpillar's head.

The caterpillar's real eyes are small and not very frightening, but the eyespots look like the huge eyes of a much larger creature. Some caterpillars can puff up the eyespot area and move it from side to side so that it looks almost like a snake's head. The staring "eyes" and snake-like movement often fool birds and insects and frighten them away.

Caterpillars have many ways of defending themselves, but they are not always able to escape their enemies. Predators such as birds, frogs, toads, spiders, and insects are constantly looking for juicy caterpillars to eat or to feed to their young.

Some insects have a special way of using caterpillars as a source of food. Certain kinds of wasps deposit their eggs inside the bodies of caterpillars. The wasp larvae that hatch from the eggs feed on the caterpillar's tissues and organs. As the wasp larvae grow inside its body, the caterpillar becomes weaker until it finally dies. Then the wasp larvae emerge ready to continue their development.

Sometimes the caterpillar lives long enough to become a pupa. The wasp larvae remain inside its body, where they enter the pupal stage of their own development. The butterfly pupa dies, while its unwelcome guests develop into adult wasps.

This female wasp is getting ready to deposit her eggs inside the body of a swallowtail caterpillar.

Large numbers of butterfly caterpillars are killed by wasps and other predators. But many survive to reach the fifth and final stage of their development.

A fifth-instar caterpillar eats constantly, just like the other instars. But one day, it suddenly stops eating. The time has come for the larva to enter the next stage of metamorphosis and become a pupa.

A swallowtail caterpillar gets ready for this transformation by attaching itself to a branch or twig. To do this, it spins silk threads that encircle its body and connect it to the twig.

This swallowtail caterpillar is preparing for the pupal stage by spinning silk thread to hold itself onto a twig.

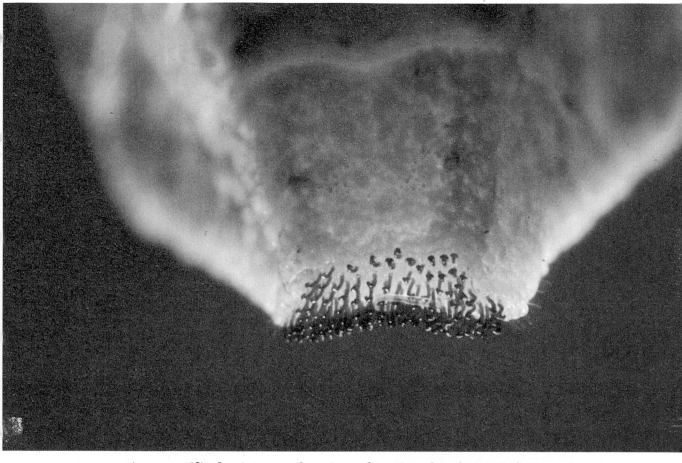

A magnified picture showing the tiny hooks on the anal prolegs that help to hold the caterpillar on the twig

These threads will hold it safely in place while the transformation takes place. The caterpillar has another method of fastening itself to the twig. It holds on with its anal prolegs, located on the last segment of its abdomen. Once it is secure, not even a strong wind will be able to blow it down.

The caterpillar sheds
its crumpled skin.

Fastened to its twig, the caterpillar sheds its skin for the last time. The old skin is pushed off like crumpled brown paper, revealing the soft body of the **pupa** underneath. Soon a hard shell, called a **chrysalis,** forms around the pupa. Within this shell an amazing change will take place. The fat, clumsy caterpillar will be transformed into a beautiful adult butterfly.

This transformation may take only a few days or many months to be completed. Different species require different amounts of time. Weather conditions also play a part in the timing of a butterfly's development. Some swallowtails that live in northern countries lay their eggs in late summer. The caterpillars that hatch from the eggs become pupae near the end of autumn. Instead of developing into adult butterflies right away, these pupae go into **hibernation** for the winter.

During hibernation, the activities of the pupa's body slow down, and metamorphosis stops. The picture on this page shows a pupa in hibernation. It has an especially thick shell that provides protection during the cold winter months. The brown color of the shell makes it look like a dry, crumpled leaf. This disguise will help to protect the pupa from predators.

Hidden in its shell, the pupa continues to hibernate until early spring. With the warmer temperatures, it will come out of hibernation, and the process of the metamorphosis will begin where it stopped in the autumn.

A butterfly pupa enclosed in a green chrysalis. Perched on the chrysalis is a small green-worm wasp. Wasps of this species use butterfly larvae and pupae as food for their young.

Other swallowtails go through metamorphosis more quickly. They begin life as eggs in late spring and develop into adult butterflies during the summer. In their pupal stage, these swallowtails have green shells that blend in with the green summer leaves.

The pictures on these two pages show a swallowtail pupa in the last stage of its development.

As the pupa hangs suspended from its twig, great changes take place inside its shell. The fat, segmented body of the larva is transformed into the slender, three-part body of an adult butterfly. The larva's system of muscles is completely rearranged, and wings grow out of its sides. The caterpillar's six simple eyes are replaced by two large compound eyes. The first three pairs of caterpillar legs develop into the long, thin legs of the adult butterfly.

As the pupa develops, the chrysalis begins to change in color and thickness. Near the end of the pupal stage, the adult insect forming inside can be seen as if through frosted glass. The long, slender body and brightly marked wings are developed and waiting to emerge.

A sallow swallowtail chrysalis splits open, and the adult butterfly slowly begins to emerge.

At last metamorphosis is complete, and it is time for the adult butterfly to emerge. The chrysalis splits apart behind the insect's head. Slowly, the butterfly begins to work its way out. First, it pushes its legs and antennae through the opening. The butterfly stretches its legs upward, searching for a firm platform. Leaving its shell behind, the insect crawls out onto the branch. It hangs there quietly, resting after its hard work.

At first, its body and wings are very wet. The body looks fat, and the wings are crumpled. The butterfly clings to the branch, drying out in the air and sunshine. Then it begins to pump blood from its body into the veins of its wings. The wings unfold and expand. In about half an hour, they are completely expanded, and the butterfly is a fully formed adult.

The newly emerged butterfly clings to a twig. Its empty chrysalis is still attached to the branch below.

As soon as its wings have expanded and dried, the swallowtail is ready to begin its life as an adult butterfly. It flies off to find its first meal of nectar or to search for a mate. Its wings will soon become faded and torn, but at this moment, they are perfect—brilliantly colored, with every scale in place. The tiny creature that began its development inside the egg has reached the final stage of its life cycle. During the next few weeks, it will mate and produce the eggs that will begin a new cycle of development and a new generation of butterflies.

GLOSSARY

abdomen—the back section of a butterfly's or caterpillar's body. The last nine segments of a caterpillar's body make up its abdomen.

antenna—a sense organ on the head of an insect. The plural form of the word is *antennae* (an-TEN-ee).

caterpillar—the special name for the larva of a butterfly or moth

chrysalis (KRIS-uh-lis)—the shell that forms around the pupa of a butterfly

crochets (kro-SHAYS)—curved spines or hooks on the prolegs of caterpillars

hibernate—to spend the winter in a state of inactivity during which all body functions are slowed down

instar—one of several stages or forms in a caterpillar's development

larva—the second stage of metamorphosis, in which the insect is wingless and worm-like. The plural form of the word is *larvae* (LAR-vee).

metamorphosis (met-uh-MOR-fuh-sis)—the process of development that produces an adult butterfly. During metamorphosis, the insect goes through four complete changes in form: egg, larva, pupa, adult

molting—shedding an old skin to make way for a new one

nectar (NECK-tuhr)—a sweet substance produced by flowers that butterflies use as food

46

osmeterium (oz-meh-TER-ee-um)—an organ on the heads of swallowtail caterpillars that gives off an unpleasant odor. It is used for defense against predators.

pigment—a chemical that produces color

predator—an animal that kills and eats another animal

proboscis (pruh-BAHS-uhs)—a long tube extending from the mouth of a butterfly, used to suck nectar and water

prolegs—stumpy legs located on the middle segments and the last segment of a caterpillar's body

protective coloring—coloring on an insect's body that helps it to blend into its surroundings

pupa (PEW-puh)—the third stage of metamorphosis, during which the larva changes into an adult butterfly. The plural form of the word is *pupae* (PEW-pee).

scales—tiny, ridged plates arranged in overlapping fashion on the surfaces of a butterfly's wings

spermatophore (sper-MAT-uh-fore)—a compact packet of sperm passed from a male butterfly's body to the female's body during mating

spinneret (spin-uh-RET)—a tube through which silk emerges from a caterpillar's body

spiracles (SPEAR-uh-kuhls)—breathing holes on an insect's body

thorax—the middle section of a butterfly's or caterpillar's body. The first three segments of a caterpillar's body make up its thorax.

INDEX